Ins... And Tl... ...py

Written by Quentin Flynn

Illustrated by Brent Putze

Contents Page

Rigby

Inspector Grub And The Fizzer-X Spy

With these characters . . .

Officer Clarke

Inspector Grub

Officer Murphy

Ferdinand Fezzaro

The Managers

The Researchers

Mr. Dittworthy

“He knew he had all the

He just

Setting the scene . . .

The formula for a top-secret new soft-drink has been mysteriously smuggled out of the research laboratory. No one knows who the spy is—or how he or she is managing to get the complex formula out of the laboratory. At first, there seem to be no clues—and even with Inspector Grub and his two officers working undercover, the case seems too hard to solve. Will the clever spy be able to get away with it? Or will the inspector be able to see what no one else can?

clues to solve the spy hunt.
needed to sort them out."

Chapter 1.

Mr. Ferdinand Fezzaro's eyes bulged in alarm. As he sat behind his huge, polished desk, his heart pounded. He stared at the object that upset him.

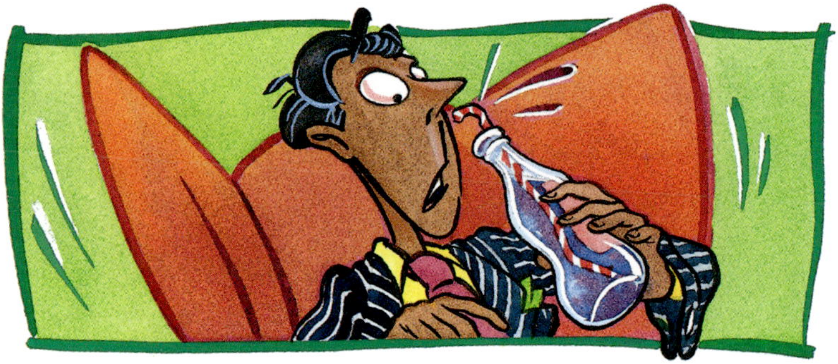

"How could they have done that?" he said to himself. He reached out and picked up the object. It was a small, opened bottle of soda pop. He lifted it to his nostrils and took another sniff. He raised it to his lips and took another sip. He sighed a very worried sigh, and called his personal assistant into the room.

"Miss Harbinger, please call an emergency meeting of the managers. We have an extremely serious problem."

Later that afternoon, the managers of Fezzaro and Flummox High-Quality Soft-Drink Manufacturers sat attentively around the table. Ferdinand Fezzaro rose slowly from his chair and spoke to his colleagues.

"As you all know, we have been working for almost a year on our new, top-secret soft-drink, code-named Fizzer-X. I am afraid I have to tell you that our main competitor has beaten us to it."

"This morning, I bought *this* bottle of soft-drink at a convenience store."

He placed the bottle on the table.

"It tastes just like Fizzer-X. It bubbles just like Fizzer-X. It smells just like Fizzer-X. In fact, if I didn't know better, I'd say it *was* Fizzer-X!"

The managers were shocked. They didn't know what to say. They passed the bottle around, sniffing and staring at it.

"But how can this happen?" asked one of the managers. "We have the tightest security in our research laboratory. No one is allowed to leave the building with any formula notes or samples of the drink. Everyone is searched by our security guards when they arrive. Everyone is sniffed by our sniffer dogs when they leave the research laboratory. How could someone smuggle out our complex, top-secret formula?"

"That is what we need to find out," said Ferdinand Fezzaro. "If we have a spy in our midst, we need to hunt him, or her, down quickly!"

The managers were amazed that a spy could be working somewhere in their company. They muttered and murmured, shook their heads, and sighed. Ferdinand Fezzaro tapped the competitor's bottle with his pencil.

"Unfortunately, we can trust no-one," he said gravely. "We need a clever detective, Miss Harbinger. Call Inspector Grub."

Chapter 2.

Inspector Grub burped loudly.

"I beg your pardon," he apologized, looking embarrassed. "It's very fizzy," he said, putting down the bottle of Fizzer-X on his desk.

Ferdinand Fezzaro frowned at the bottle. Officers Clarke and Murphy sat on either side of him writing in their notebooks.

"Should I have written 'burp' down?" whispered Officer Clarke to Officer Murphy. Inspector Grub heard him and glared. Officer Clark swiftly scribbled out the word "burp".

Inspector Grub licked his lips. "So we have a spy-hunt on our hands," he said. "We will need a list of everybody who works in your research laboratory, Mr. Fezzaro."

Ferdinand Fezzaro nodded. "I will phone Miss Harbinger and ask her to print out a list for you immediately."

"And we will need to conduct our investigation without alerting the spy. If he or she thinks we are suspicious, they will become even harder to catch."

Inspector Grub continued, “Officer Clarke. Officer Murphy. Go home and change out of your uniforms. We need to work undercover. We will disguise ourselves as soft-drink manufacturers returning from a vacation in Polynesia.”

An hour later, Inspector Grub and Ferdinand Fezzaro waited for the two officers outside the police station. Inspector Grub wore a suit with a soft-drink logo on the jacket pocket.

When Officer Murphy walked around the corner, the inspector groaned. But when Officer Clarke walked around the corner, the inspector was flabbergasted!

Both were dressed in their brightest shorts and flowered shirts. But Officer Clarke looked *very* strange.

"These are the best undercover clothes we could find," explained Officer Murphy.

"And I'm disguised as a woman," said Officer Clarke in a high-pitched voice. He winked at Inspector Grub, who just groaned again.

"You're supposed to look inconspicuous, not ridiculous," muttered Inspector Grub. He looked them up and down and sighed. "Oh, well, let's get started."

Ferdinand Fezzaro drove the inspector and his officers to the Fezzaro and Flummox factory. After they were searched by the security guards, Ferdinand Fezzaro showed them through the research laboratory.

There were rows of shiny steel laboratory benches with beakers, test tubes, and rubber pipes full of liquids bubbling and fizzing away. There were jars of spices, bottles of juice, and bowls of fruit everywhere. There were rows of bottles of bright food coloring. There were bags of brown sugar, white sugar, and raw sugar.

Three people in white coats moved around the benches staring intently at the ingredients and the laboratory equipment and writing notes on small clipboards. Ferdinand Fezzaro introduced the visiting soft-drink manufacturers to the researchers. They looked strangely at Officer Clarke, nodded at the other two police officers, and went back to their research work.

“This is where our secret formulas are developed,” explained Ferdinand Fezzaro. “Apart from the managers, only these three people know what goes into our soft-drinks.”

“Very good, Mr. Fezzaro. That’s how we do things too,” said Inspector Grub in an odd accent.

Ferdinand Fezzaro checked that no one was watching and handed Inspector Grub the list of names.

"Hans Grobble, Maria Spitz, and Janet Dribbel. Our three researchers." He pointed out each person. "But our formulas are very complex, and no one is allowed to leave this room with any notes or paper from the laboratory."

"Yes, yes," said Officer Clarke in his highest, loudest voice. He was enjoying being in disguise. "As we say ourselves, 'top-secret is better than *not*-secret'!"

He lowered his voice and whispered to Ferdinand Fezzaro. "Could Grobble, Spitz, or Dribbel have simply memorized the formula?" he asked.

"There are so many ingredients, in such exact quantities, that even I can't remember them all," replied Ferdinand Fezzaro, eyeing the researchers. "Someone must be writing the formulas down and getting them out somehow. But with no paper and no notes, how is it being done?"

Chapter 3.

Inspector Grub looked around the room. There were no windows, so the researchers couldn't pass anything to the outside of the laboratory. There were no telephones, so they couldn't read the formulas over the phone.

"Write down everything that you see on the benches," he whispered to Officers Clarke and Murphy.

The two police officers tried to look inconspicuous as they moved around the laboratory, glancing at the benches and fumbling with their notebooks. Officer Clarke's wig flopped over his eyes.

Inspector Grub groaned. "How did those two ever become police officers?" he asked under his breath. Just then, as Officer Murphy tried to slip inconspicuously past a desk, he knocked a bowl of lemons onto the floor.

Janet Dribbel, the nearest researcher, rushed over and started to pick them up.

"T-t-terribly sorry," stammered Officer Murphy. "I'm so clumsy! I hope you didn't need them for your experiment."

"No, no," sniffed Dribbel. "We don't use lemons in our formulas. These are mine. I have a terrible cold, and I've been drinking hot lemon juice every day."

Janet Dribbel sneezed loudly into her handkerchief. "Obviously, the lemons are not helping my cold much," she said grumpily, sniffing again.

Officers Murphy and Clarke finished their inspection and returned to Inspector Grub and Ferdinand Fezzaro, who stood in the corridor.

"Nothing unusual to report," said Officer Murphy. "Only laboratory equipment, a few ballpoint pens, a few fountain pens, some pencils and some blank notepaper. Even the trashcans are empty."

"Same here. Nothing unusual," agreed Officer Clarke. "Except Hans Grobble winked at me twice!"

Then Inspector Grub had a sudden idea.

"Mr. Fezzaro," he said. "They are not the only people who go into that room, are they? Somebody else has access to the top-secret laboratory. Somebody the security guards don't check. Somebody who comes in at night, and who can easily copy formulas or remove notes hidden in the trashcans without being seen."

Mr. Fezzaro raised his eyebrows. "Who?" he asked.

Inspector Grub folded his arms. "Mr. Fezzaro, who *cleans* this room?"

Ferdinand Fezzaro smiled and shook his head. "No, Inspector Grub, that would be impossible. Every evening, I lock the formulas away in a safe. There is nothing left on the desks. And *that*," he said pointing to a machine in the corner of the laboratory, "is a shredder. All paper that has been written on is shredded in the machine before everyone leaves."

"Hmmm," said Inspector Grub. "I'm still not convinced. I want to set a trap for this cleaning person. Unlikely as it may be, the cleaning person is our most obvious suspect."

Ferdinand Fezzaro shrugged. "OK," he said. "I'll arrange for Miss Harbinger to fax you the name of the cleaning person and the hours that he works."

Back at the police station later that day, Inspector Grub issued instructions to the officers. He read from the page he had just taken from the fax machine.

“The cleaning person name is Mr. Dittworthy. He finishes work at 8:00 P.M. I want you two waiting outside the laboratory the moment he comes out. And when he does, I want you to swoop down on his cleaning cart. Investigate everything that is on it. If there’s even the slightest hint of a formula, recipe, or list of ingredients, I want to know about it immediately.”

The two officers nodded enthusiastically. "Yes, sir!" they said together. At last, the spy-hunt was getting exciting.

"And another thing," said Inspector Grub to the two police officers waiting expectantly, "my eyes are getting sore just looking at you. Change out of those ridiculous clothes!" he roared.

Chapter 4.

Inspector Grub waited impatiently in his office as night fell. He ate all his snacks and drank three cups of tea. He checked his watch over and over again: 7:45 P.M.; 7:50 P.M.; 7:55 P.M. As soon as the phone rang, Inspector Grub grabbed the receiver.

"Well?" he asked. "What did you find?"

"We apprehended Mr. Dittworthy, just as you asked," replied Officer Clarke. "He was a little bit annoyed," he added sheepishly.

"What did you find on his cart?" asked Inspector Grub urgently. He heard Officer Clarke flicking through his notebook.

"The suspect was in possession of one cleaning cart," he began to read. "On the suspect's cart were three blue rags, two detergent bottles, one bottle of bleach, a toilet brush, and one sheet of crumpled paper," reported Officer Clarke.

"*A-ha!*" said Inspector Grub triumphantly. "And what was on the paper, as if I can't guess?"

There was silence on the other end of the phone line.

"Well?" asked the inspector, smiling to himself. "Formulas, by any chance? Secret ingredients for top-secret soft-drinks?" He folded his arms and the tips of his moustache twitched.

"Actually, Inspector," replied Officer Clarke, "the paper was blank."

Blank paper in trashcans? *Blank* paper. That was *most* mysterious! Inspector Grub sat with his feet on his desk staring out his window. He knew he had all the clues required to solve the spy hunt. He just needed to sort them out.

Images kept spinning around in his head like clothes in a washing machine: Officer Clarke's floppy wig, Officer Murphy's bathing trunks, bags of sugar, bowls of lemons, beakers and test tubes, burps, bottles of bleach, and blank pieces of paper. He just couldn't see how it all worked together. He couldn't *see* it.

Instantly, he sat up straight, eyes bright and opened wide. He nodded his head.

"I should have known! That was it!" shouted Inspector Grub.

The inspector leaped up and grabbed the phone. The Fizzer-X spy mystery was solved!

"You and Officer Clarke will meet me at 8:00 A.M. tomorrow morning at Fezzaro and Flummox," he ordered Officer Murphy. "And bring your handcuffs. Both of you!"

Chapter 5.

Everyone was assembled in the research laboratory of Fezzaro and Flummox. Grobble, Spitz, and Dribbel, the three researchers, were looking around nervously. Mr. Dittworthy, who was leaning on his cart, seemed to be in a very bad mood. He wasn't due to start work for hours yet. Ferdinand Fezzaro looked bewildered. Officers Clarke and Murphy looked grimly from face to face. They had no idea what was about to happen either, but they hoped that no one realized this.

"Thank you all for coming," said the inspector. "This morning, we are going to arrest the Fizzer-X spy." The group gasped. Everyone looked at each other suspiciously. Who was the spy?

Inspector Grub fished around in his jacket pocket and brought out a piece of blank paper. He flattened it out on one of the benches and looked at every person in the room.

"What is on this piece of paper?" he asked.

Everyone stared at the blank piece of paper.

"I can't see anything," replied one of the researchers.

"There's nothing on it," said another.

"Mr. Dittworthy, would you mind bringing me a bottle of your bleach?" asked Inspector Grub politely.

Inspector Grub poured a small amount of the bleach in a bowl, and added some water. Then he placed the blank piece of paper in the bowl and gently washed the bleach mixture over it.

Slowly, patches of dark brown appeared on the paper, as if by magic. The patches turned into lines and squiggles. Everyone gasped as the patches turned into writing.

The inspector turned to Janet Dribbel, the researcher with the cold.

"Perhaps," he said, "you might tell us what this says?"

Janet Dribbel's face turned bright red as she read the writing on the paper. "It says 'Clever, but not clever enough,'" she groaned miserably.

Back at the station, Inspector Grub explained how the crime had been committed.

"The spy—or should I say, spies—used invisible ink to pass the formulas out of the laboratory. Dribbel didn't really have a cold, but she squeezed fresh lemon juice for her hot lemon drink every day. Only *some* of it went into her drink. She used the rest as invisible ink to write down the exact quantities of each secret ingredient on a piece of paper. Of course, no one could see what she had written."

"Every evening, Mr. Dittworthy would take the top sheet of her notebook. No one would look twice at a crumpled, blank piece of paper on a cleaning cart. Once outside the laboratory, all he had to do was wash a little bleach over the page, and presto! The lemon juice and the bleach mixture reacted, revealing the formula in clear brown writing. That top-secret formula was then ready to be sold to the competing soft-drink company."

"Bravo!" clapped Ferdinand Fezzaro. Everyone else smiled at Inspector Grub. He really was the most clever detective around. Ferdinand Fezzaro beckoned to Miss Harbinger, who began passing around a huge crate of Fizzer-X.

"Drink up!" he beamed to everyone at the police station. "We're canceling the Fizzer-X project and starting work on a new top-secret lemon-flavored drink straight away."

He turned toward Inspector Grub. "And you've given us an idea for the perfect name. We'll call it the *In-fizz-able Drink*!"

“A spy’s on the loose!”

A spy’s
on the
loose!
Flowered
shirts and
lemon juice!
Bring in the
inspector, watch
out for the bubbles;
Our secret is stolen;
Can Grub solve
our troubles?
Let him think!
Let him think!
Cleaning carts,
bleach and fizzy drink!
How are the secrets
getting through?
Will our man
find the culprit
before *you* do?